THE LIFE CYCLE OF A
Butterfly

By Colleen Sexton

BELLWETHER MEDIA · MINNEAPOLIS, MN

Note to Librarians, Teachers, and Parents:

Blastoff! Readers are carefully developed by literacy experts and combine standards-based content with developmentally appropriate text.

Level 1 provides the most support through repetition of high-frequency words, light text, predictable sentence patterns, and strong visual support.

Level 2 offers early readers a bit more challenge through varied simple sentences, increased text load, and less repetition of high-frequency words.

Level 3 advances early-fluent readers toward fluency through increased text and concept load, less reliance on visuals, longer sentences, and more literary language.

Level 4 builds reading stamina by providing more text per page, increased use of punctuation, greater variation in sentence patterns, and increasingly challenging vocabulary.

Level 5 encourages children to move from "learning to read" to "reading to learn" by providing even more text, varied writing styles, and less familiar topics.

Whichever book is right for your reader, Blastoff! Readers are the perfect books to build confidence and encourage a love of reading that will last a lifetime!

This edition first published in 2010 by Bellwether Media, Inc.

No part of this publication may be reproduced in whole or in part without written permission of the publisher. For information regarding permission, write to Bellwether Media, Inc., Attention: Permissions Department, 5357 Penn Avenue South, Minneapolis, MN 55419.

Library of Congress Cataloging-in-Publication Data
Sexton, Colleen A., 1967–
  The life cycle of a butterfly / by Colleen Sexton.
    p. cm. — (Blastoff! Readers life cycles)
  Includes bibliographical references and index.
  Summary: "Developed by literacy experts for students in kindergarten through grade three, this book follows butterflies as they transform from eggs to adults. Through leveled text and related images, young readers will watch these creatures grow through every stage of life"–Provided by publisher.
  ISBN 978-1-60014-306-9 (hardcover : alk. paper)
  1. Butterflies–Life cycles–Juvenile literature. I. Title.
  QL544.2.S453 2010
  595.78'9–dc22
                                          2009037216

Text copyright © 2010 by Bellwether Media, Inc. BLASTOFF! READERS and associated logos are trademarks and/or registered trademarks of Bellwether Media, Inc.

Printed in the United States of America, North Mankato MN.
010110   1149

Contents

What Are Butterflies?   4

The Egg Stage   7

The Larva Stage   8

The Pupa Stage   18

The Adult Stage   19

Glossary   22

To Learn More   23

Index   24

Butterflies are **insects**. They live everywhere but the hottest and coldest places on Earth.

There are more than 15,000 kinds of butterflies. This butterfly is a **monarch**.

Butterflies grow in stages. The stages of a butterfly's **life cycle** are egg, **larva**, **pupa**, and adult.

egg

larva

pupa

adult

A male butterfly and a female butterfly **mate**. The female is then ready to lay eggs. She finds a plant and places her eggs on it.

A larva grows inside an egg. A butterfly larva is called a **caterpillar**.

Soon the caterpillar is ready to hatch.
It chews its way out of the egg and
eats the whole shell.

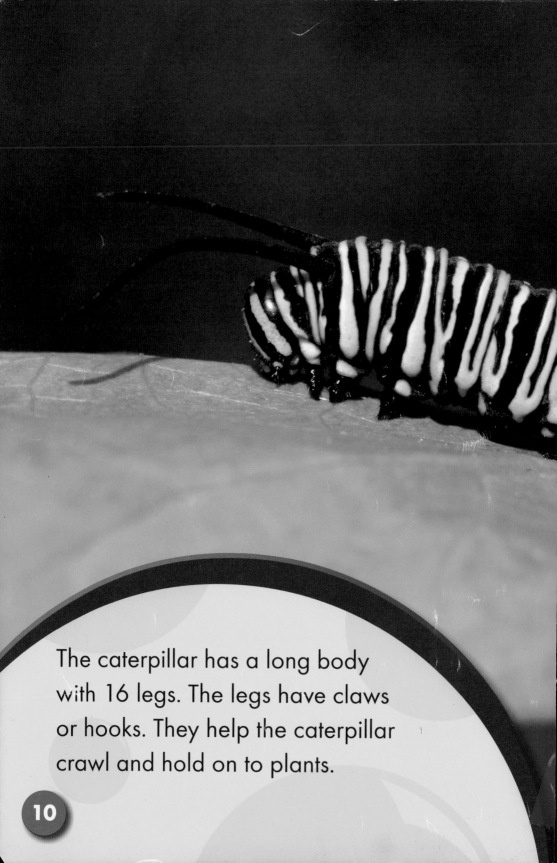

The caterpillar has a long body with 16 legs. The legs have claws or hooks. They help the caterpillar crawl and hold on to plants.

The caterpillar has strong jaws for chewing leaves. It spends all its time eating and grows quickly.

The caterpillar grows so much that its skin becomes tight. The caterpillar is ready to **molt**.

Its skin splits open. The caterpillar crawls out of its old skin. Its new skin soon hardens.

The caterpillar eats, grows, and molts again. It molts four or five times.

The caterpillar is now fully grown. It looks for a safe place to rest.

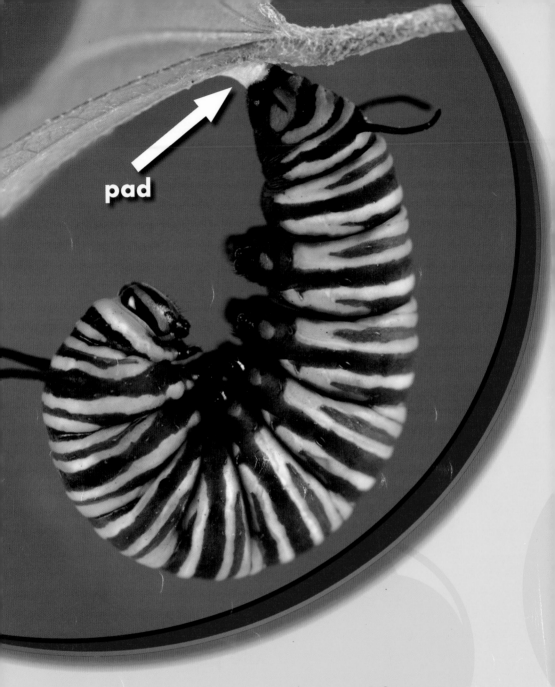

pad

The caterpillar drops sticky liquid from its body onto its resting spot. The liquid hardens into a pad.

The caterpillar hooks its back pair of legs into the pad and hangs upside down.

The caterpillar's skin splits open and falls away.
The caterpillar has changed into a pupa.

A hard case called a **chrysalis** covers
the pupa. The pupa changes into an adult
butterfly inside the chrysalis.

The new butterfly breaks out of the chrysalis. It stretches its damp wings until they are flat.

Now the butterfly is ready to fly! It will mate and a new life cycle will begin.

Glossary

caterpillar—the larva of a butterfly

chrysalis—the hard case in which a pupa turns into a butterfly; the chrysalis protects the pupa.

insect—a small animal with six legs and a body divided into three parts; there are more insects in the world than any other kind of animal.

larva—a young insect that hatches from an egg and looks like a small worm; the larva is the second stage of a butterfly's life.

life cycle—the stages of life of an animal; a life cycle includes being born, growing up, having young, and dying.

mate—to join together to produce young

molt—to shed skin so that new skin can grow

monarch—a large orange and black butterfly that lives in North America and many other parts of the world

pupa—the third stage of an insect's life when it turns from a larva into an adult; a butterfly pupa changes inside a chrysalis.

To Learn More

AT THE LIBRARY

Huseby, Victoria. *Butterfly*. Mankato, Minn.: Smart Apple Media, 2009.

Kalman, Bobbie. *Animal Life Cycles: Growing and Changing*. New York, N.Y.: Crabtree Publishing, 2006.

Rustad, Martha E.H. *Butterflies*. Minneapolis, Minn.: Bellwether Media, 2008.

ON THE WEB

Learning more about life cycles is as easy as 1, 2, 3.

1. Go to www.factsurfer.com.

2. Enter "life cycles" into the search box.

3. Click the "Surf" button and you will see a list of related Web sites.

With factsurfer.com, finding more information is just a click away.

Index

adult, 6, 19

caterpillar, 8, 9, 10,
    11, 12, 13, 14, 15,
    16, 17, 18

chrysalis, 19, 20

Earth, 4

egg, 6, 7, 8, 9

insects, 4

jaws, 11

larva, 6, 8

life cycle, 6, 21

mating, 7, 21

molting, 12, 13, 14

monarch, 5

pad, 16, 17

pupa, 6, 18, 19

skin, 12, 13, 18

wings, 20

The images in this book are reproduced through the courtesy of: Cathy Keifer, front cover (adult, larva, pupa), pp. 6 (adult, larva, pupa), 9, 13, 18-19, 20; Papilio / Alamy, front cover (egg), pp. 6 (egg), 8; Goran Kapor, pp. 4, 21; Doug Lemke, p. 5; Rick & Nora Bowers / Alamy, p. 7; Martin Shields / Alamy, pp. 10-11; Ron Brancato, p. 12; Dwight Kuhn, p. 14; Juan Martinez, p. 15; Brandon Alms, p. 16; T Kitchin & V Hurst, p. 17.